Dear ________________,

____

____

From,

____

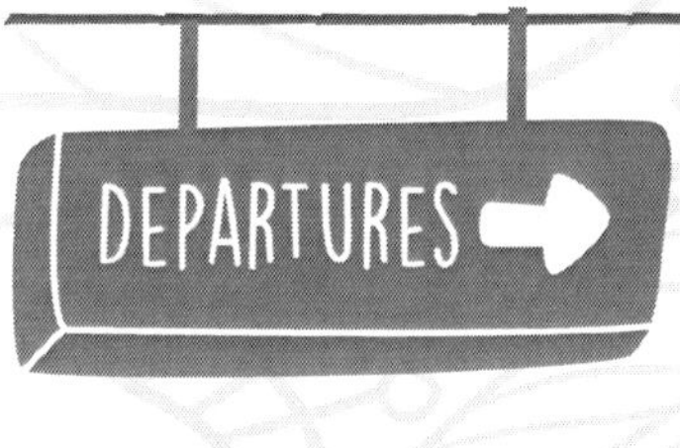

First of all, let's thank our Aviation Industry and all it's employees for making our lives so much easier. Whether you're a pilot, a frequent traveler, or just someone who happens to be really into aviation, airplane jokes are undoubtedly the best to laugh out loud. The constipation-inducing food, the negative legroom, the delays, re-routes, and cancellations can sometimes make air travel a bit hectic but nothing puts you in a better mood than a silly joke. Which is why we've gone ahead and rounded up these 100 funniest aviation jokes and puns to keep you entertained for a while. ENJOY!

Interviewer: How often do these things crash?

Pilot: Usually, just once.

Son: Dad, when I grow up I want to be a pilot.

Dad: Sorry son, you can't do both.

Q: What is the difference between a co pilot and a duck?

A: A duck knows how to fly.

As soon as the stewardess serves the coffee, the airplane encounters turbulence.

Did you know that the propeller on a small plane is actaully there to keep the pilot cool?

When it stops spinning, the pilot starts sweating like crazy.

Q: How do you know if there is a pilot in the room?

A: He will already have told you.

A businessman was having a tough time lugging his lumpy, oversized travel bag onto the plane. Helped by a flight attendant, he finally managed to stuff it in the overhead bin.

"Do you always carry such heavy luggage?" she sighed. "No more," the man said. "Next time, I'm riding in the bag, and my partner can buy the ticket!"

Q: What do doctors and pilots have in common?

A: They both wanted to be pilots when they were growing up.

Q: What is the difference between a jet engine and a co-pilot?

A: The jet engine stops whining when the plane shuts down.

The 3 things you don't want to hear in a cockpit:

Flight engineer: "That's odd..."

First officer: "I have an idea."

Captain: "Watch this!"

On landing, the Stewardess said, “Please be sure to take all of your belongings. If you're going to leave anything, please make sure it's something we'd like to have”

The attendant at the Airlines check-in desk asked, "Window or Aisle?"

I replied, "Window or you'll what?"

Q: What should a pilot never say in a job interview?

A: I am down to earth.

Q: What do you call a black pilot?

A: a pilot, you racist.

Interviewer: What made you become a pilot?

Pilot: I had to defy my biggest fear.

Interviewer: Heights?

Pilot: No, dying alone.

First day as a pilot:

Control tower: Can you give me your position?

Me: I am next to a cloud that looks like a lion.

Control tower: Can you be more specific?

Me: Simba.

Q: What do you call it when you're sick of being in the airport?

A: Terminal illness.

A pilot should never go homeless...

Because then he's going to look for a place to crash.

2 pilots met...

300 people died.

Q: How do you know you are halfway through a date with a pilot?

A: He will say "enough about flying, lets talk about me."

It was mealtime on an airplane, and the flight attendant asked a passenger if he would like some dinner.

"What are my choices?" the passenger asked.

"Yes or no," she replied.

Right after take off, a pilot comes on the microphone to welcome his passengers. “Thank you for flying with us. The weather is....”

Then he suddenly starts screaming while still on the mic, “OH MY GOD! IT IS BURNING!!, IT IS BURNING!”

Then silence.

A few seconds later, he comes back on and says, “I'm terribly sorry about what happened. I spilled some scorching hot coffee on my lap... you should see my pants!!”

A voice from the back of the plane yells, “Why don't you come here and see ours?”

Give a man a plane ticket, he'll fly for a day...

Push a man out of a plane, he'll fly for the rest of his life.

So I'm making a TV series about a plane hijacking...

We've just shot the pilot.

Q: Why did the pilot get sent to his room?

A: Bad altitude.

I was woken on the plane by a panicky stewardess...

That's how i lost my job as a pilot.

As an aspiring actor, I was somewhat surprised when I got detained by airport security today...

All I said was that I was in town to shoot a pilot.

I don't find airplane jokes funny.

To me they're just really boeing.

Q: What did the kamikaze pilot tell his students?

A: Watch closely. I'm only gonna show this once.

A pilot is making an announcement to his passengers:

"We got some good news, and some bad news. The good news is that you guys will be on TV tonight!"

Japan's worst kamikaze pilot...

He flew over 25 missions.

My uncle used to always say, "it's the journey not the destination that matters".

Nice guy, horrible pilot.

Q: Why did the sitcom about airplanes never take off?

A: Because the pilot was terrible.

Pilot John John, age 85, died peacefully in his sleep last Tuesday.

The rest of his passengers weren't so lucky...

Q: Why did the pilot feel insecure?

A: His job was always up in the air.

Q: Why were the flight attendants panicked when someone decided to leave work an hour early?

A: Because it was the pilot.

Q: Why did the airplane pilot decide to retire?

A: Because it was too Boeing.

Q: Why are pilots never charged with speeding tickets?

A: Because they fly above the law.

Q: What illness do pilots get the most?

A: The flew.

Q: Where does a mountain climber keep his plane?

A: In a cliff-hangar.

Q: Why do people take an instant dislike to flight attendants?

A: To save time later.

Q: Will invisible airplanes ever be a thing?

A: I just can't see them taking off.

Q: How many pilots does it take to change a lightbulb?

A: Just one, he holds the lightbulb and the earth rotates around him.

I asked a flight attendant to change my seat because of a crying baby next to me...

It turns out you can't do that if the baby is yours.

A Boeing 737 Max flight attendant walks into a bar and orders a martini.

“You’re here later than usual,” the bartender comments. “Problems at work?”

“Yes, just as our flight was about to take off, we had to turn around and wait at the gate for an hour.”

“What was the problem?” the bartender asks.

“The pilot was bothered by a noise in the engine,” she replies. “It took us a while to find a new pilot.”

Q: Who invented the first airplane that wouldn't fly?

A: The Wrong Brothers.

A man telephoned an airline office in New York and asked, "How long does it take to fly to Boston?"
The clerk said, "Just a minute..."

"Thank you," the man said and hung up.

I have a really good airplane joke I want to share...

But I think it might go over your head.

Q: How does the captain know the aircraft is safely at the ramp?.

A: Both the engines and the co-pilot stop whining.

Q: What do you call an airplane that flies backward?

A: A receding airline.

Q: What happens to a bad airplane joke?

A: It never lands.

Q: What's the difference between an optimist and a pessimist?

A: An optimist created the airplane, a pessimist created the seatbelts.

Getting on a plane, I told the ticket lady, "Send one of my bags to New York, send one to Los Angeles, send one to Miami."

She said, "We can't do that!"

I told her, "You did it last week!"

Q: Why is development in airplane engineering so slow?

A: Everyone is afraid to make a groundbreaking design.

Q: How do you identify a fighter pilot at a bar?

A: You don't, he'll come up and tell you.

I tried to sue the airport for losing my luggage...

I lost my case.

Q: An ant falls out of an airplane, how did it die?

A: Starved to death on the way down.

Q: What does a person who dislikes airplane food say when he's served with chicken steak?

A: "Let's hope for the breast!"

Q: What flavour ice cream does a pilot always order?

A: Plain.

If a plane has a small crack in it, is that called an airline fracture?

Co-Pilot: (looking down):
"Sir can you tell me what these buttons do?"

Captain: "They keep your shirt closed."

"As we prepare for takeoff, please make sure your tray tables and seat backs are fully upright in their most uncomfortable position"

It is always better to be down here wishing you were up there than up there wishing you were down here.

Explaining the use of the controls to a student:

"If you push the stick forward, the houses get bigger, if you pull the stick back they get smaller...

Unless you pull the stick too far back, then the houses get bigger again very quickly."

First Day Lesson for Pilots:
"Learn from the mistakes of other pilots. You will not live long enough to make all of them yourself."

First Day Lesson for Pilots:
"Always try to keep the number of landings you make equal to the number of take offs you've made."

"Takeoffs are optional.
Landings are mandatory."

A panick-y passenger asked the air hostess if they were still traveling on the correct course.

'Off course, we are,' she replied. She couldn't understand why the passenger suffered from an anxiety attack right after that.

A man was feeling sick and dizzy on an airplane. The old lady sitting beside him noticed it and handed him some leftover peanuts to help ease his sickness. He ate them to distract himself.

After a while, when she handed him another handful of peanuts, the sick man said, 'thank you, that's very kind of you. Why don't we share these peanuts and enjoy them?'

'Oh no, I can't really eat peanuts because I don't have any teeth. But I loved sucking the sweet chocolate that covered those peanuts!'

Q: The librarian was asked to leave the plane for what reason?

A: Because it was overbooked.

Q: What makes flight attendants great astronauts?

A: They know how to take up space.

The flight was having engine trouble, and the pilot instructed the cabin crew to have the passengers take their seats and prepare for an emergency landing.

After a few minutes, the pilot asked the flight attendants if everyone was buckled in and ready.

"All set back here, Captain," came the reply, "except the lawyers are still going around passing out business cards."

The plane takes off with a two-hour delay.

In the air, a passenger asks the flight attendant: “Why did we take off so late?"

To which the flight attendant replies: “Well the pilot noticed some smoke and weird sounds coming from the plane’s left engine, and we spent a while trying to find another pilot to fly the plane.

Everyone knows that a 'good' landing is one in which you can walk away.

However, a 'great' landing is one in which you can use the airplane again afterward.

Q: Why did the pilot blush?

A: Because he saw the airstrip.

Q: How do flat-earthers travel the world?

A: On a plane.

Q: What is that situation when you're picking up your bags at the airport, and everyone's luggage is better than yours?

A: A worst case scenario.

It is impossible to play hide and seek in an airport...

Because You're always hiding in plane sight.

Never ever get on a plane if the pilot is Dutch...

He'll take off and Netherland.

Q: What sound does an airplane make when it bounces?

A: Boeing... Boeing!

A plane flies straight toward a mountain as pilot and co-pilot pull down on the control wheel with all their might

The pilot yells "We'll never make it over that mountain" the co-pilot looks at him and says "Not with that altitude."

There was a blonde sitting next to a man on an airplane. About an hour into the flight, the pilot comes on and says over the intercom, "One of our four engines is out, we will be about 15 minutes late arriving."

About 30 minutes later, the pilot comes on the intercom again and says, "There is a second engine out, we will be about 30 minutes late."

Fifteen minutes after the pilot comes on again, and says, "I'm sorry to say that we've lost our third engine, and it looks like we'll be about an hour late arriving at our destination."

The blonde turns to the man next to her and says, "Man, if that last engine goes out, we'll be up here all day."

As I sat in my airplane seat for the 16 hour flight, I tried to get comfortable...

Then I remembered that I was in economy.

Did you know that there are more airplanes underwater ...than submarines in the sky?

Did you know that airplane's black boxes are actually orange?

What? I thought they were boxes!

A concerned airplane passenger asked me if I heard about bird strikes...

I honestly didn't think they could carry signs.

The best part of being a flight attendant...

Has to be when you walk the aisle saying "trash" to everyone's face.

Q: What did the football player say to the flight attendant?

A: "Put me in coach."

Flight Attendant: Please don't forget to activate 'airplane mode'.

Me: Running around with my arms spread, making airplane noises.

A male pilot is a confused soul who talks about women when he is flying, and about flying when he is with a woman.

My hot flight attendant asked how I like my coffee

Trying to sound cool, I told her I like my coffee like I like my women.

And that's when she told me "That's cute honey, but the coffee's free. You don't have to pay for it here!"

I sleep better naked...

Why can't the flight attendant understand that?

Q: What do airplane builders say about their job?

A: "It's riveting."

Q: What happens if you wear a watch on a plane?

A: Time flies!

Q: Why did the students study in the airplane?

A: Because they were trying to get higher grades.

Q: Why did everyone scream when I held the door open for them?

A: It was in a flying plane.

Q: What is the difference between God and an airline pilot?

A: God doesn't think he's an airline pilot.

Q: What has a nose and flies, but can't smell?

A: An airplane!

Q: Why were the passengers panicked when the co-pilot greeted his friend on the flight?

A: He said, "Hi! Jack".

Woman: Can I take my dog onboard tomorrow?

Airline Desk: Sure, as long as you provide your own kennel. And it should be large enough for the dog to stand up, sit down, turn around, and roll-over.

Woman: Oh, I'll never be able to teach him all that by tomorrow!